W9-AJT-093

J
513
A1   Allington, Richard L
      Beginning to learn about numbers.

DATE DUE

SE 20 '85 NO 15		
OC 31 '85		
NO 11 '85		
DE 6 '85		
JA 17 '86		
MR 20 '86		
JY 29 '86		
OC 13 '89		
APR 24 '97		
NOV 06		

EAU CLAIRE DISTRICT LIBRARY

DEMCO

Numbers

Copyright © 1979, Raintree Publishers Inc.

All rights reserved. No part of this book may be
reproduced or utilized in any form or by any means,
electronic or mechanical, including photocopying,
recording, or by any information storage and retrieval
system, without permission in writing from the Publisher.
Inquiries should be addressed to Raintree Childrens Books,
205 West Highland Avenue, Milwaukee, Wisconsin 53203.

Library of Congress Number: 79-19200

    3 4 5 6 7 8 9 0 83 82 81

Printed in the United States of America.

Library of Congress Cataloging in Publication Data

Allington, Richard L
    Numbers.

    (Beginning to learn about)
    SUMMARY: The numerals one to ten are
introduced through a counting game, with the
correct number being determined by clues in
the illustrations.
    1.   Counting — Juvenile literature.
[1.   Counting] I.   Garcia, Tom. II.   Title.
III.   Series.
QA113.A54   513'.2   79-19200
ISBN 0-8172-1278-7 lib. bdg.

Richard L. Allington is Associate Professor, Department of Reading,
State University of New York at Albany

BEGINNING TO LEARN ABOUT

NUMBERS

BY RICHARD L. ALLINGTON, PH.D. • ILLUSTRATED BY TOM GARCIA

Raintree Childrens Books • Milwaukee • Toronto • Melbourne • London

89967

EAU CLAIRE DISTRICT LIBRARY

1

2

3

4

5

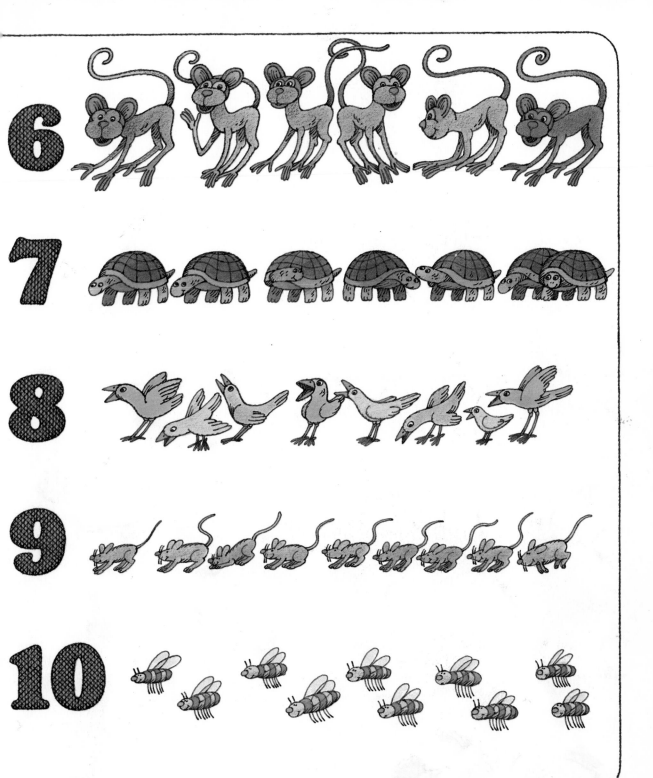

Count the fish. Then turn the page.

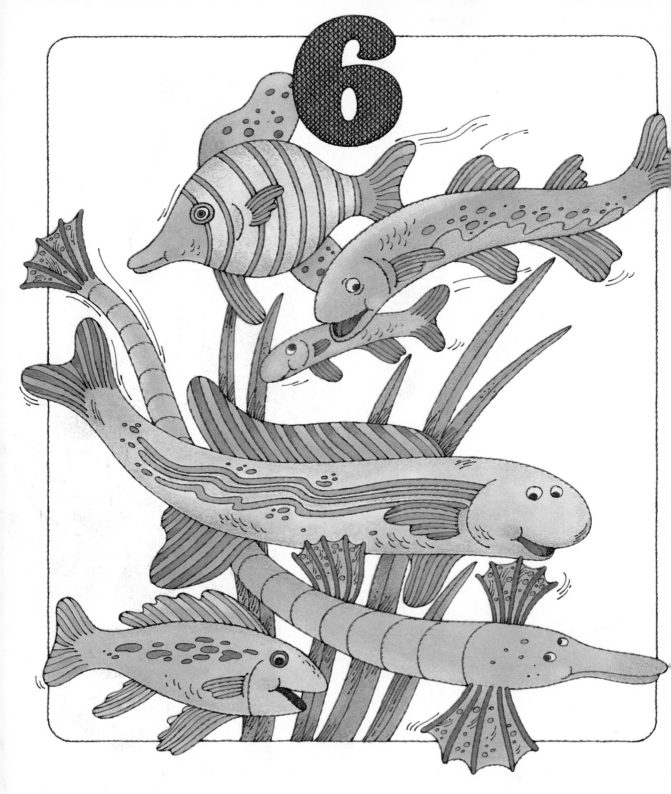

Count the dragons. Then turn the page.

10

How many elephants are behind the tree?

How many apples are in the bag?

EAU CLAIRE DISTRICT LIBRARY

How many ghosts are in the haunted house?

How many sharks are in the ocean?

How many legs does the spider have?

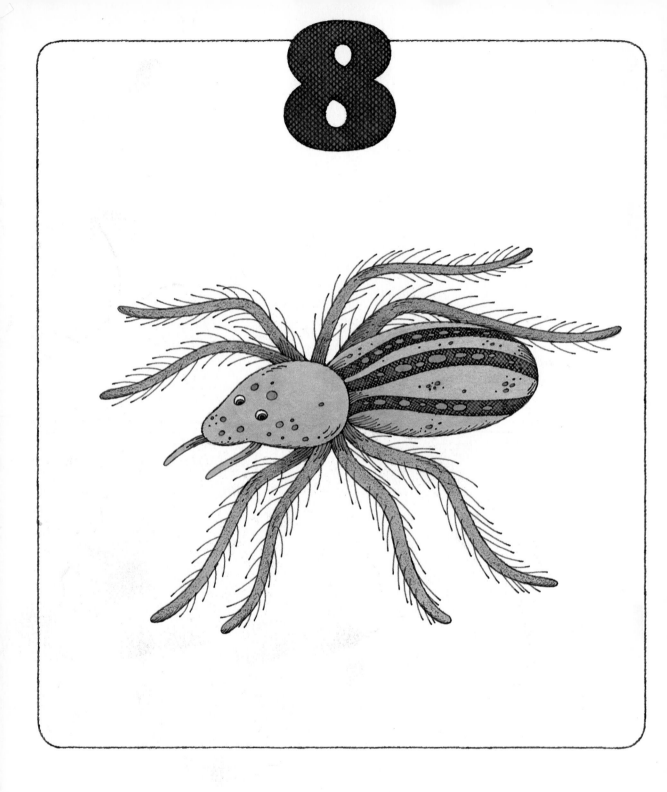

How many tigers are in the jungle?

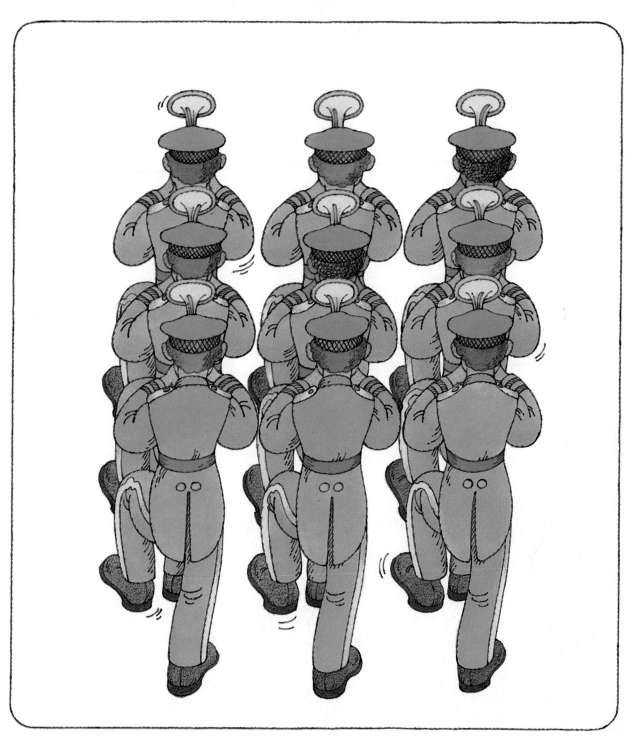

How many trumpets are in the band?

How many bees are around the flower?

Find the numerals from 1 to 9 in this picture.

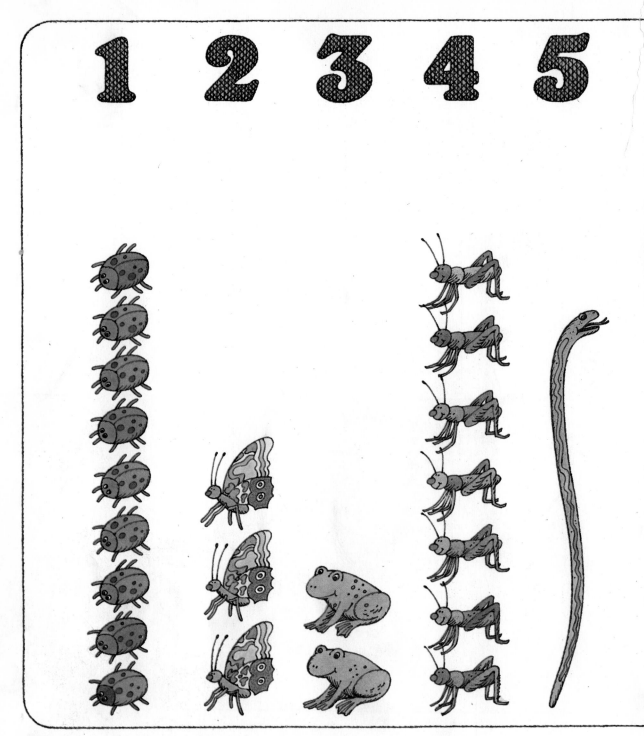

With your finger, draw a line from each numeral to the group that matches.

6 7 8 9 10

Make your own number book. Look at a newspaper or magazine. Find one of each of the numerals 1 to 10. Cut them out. Tape or paste them onto pieces of paper. Put the papers together in the right order and fasten them. You may ask an adult to help you.

———————————

Start a number collection. For each of the numerals from 1 to 10, find the matching number of objects — 10 objects to match numeral 10, 9 objects to match numeral 9, and so on. Try to find objects that have something in common. For example, start a trash number collection: 10 bottle caps, 9 pieces of old string, 8 worn-out pencils, 7 old magazines, and so on.

EAU CLAIRE DISTRICT LIBRARY.